C000065732

Children
Do Come with a
MANUAL

It is the Bible

Elizabeth Len Wai

page
vision

228 Hamilton Ave.,
Palo Alto, CA 94301

Copyright © 2024 by Elizabeth Len Wai.

ISBN 978-1-960946-57-7 (softcover)
ISBN 978-1-960946-58-4 (ebook)

All rights reserved. No part of this book may be reproduced or transmitted in any form or by any means, electronic or mechanical, including photocopying, recording, or by any information storage and retrieval system without express written permission from the author, except in the case of brief quotations embodied in critical reviews and certain other noncommercial uses permitted by copyright law.

Printed in the United States of America.

Contents

Dedication 5

Preface...7

Introduction..9

Chapter One: Every Child Is a Gift................................11

Chapter Two: Why am I here?.....................................15

Chapter Three: The Trinity and Helping Children Understand It 19

Chapter Four: Power Of The Spirit 23

Chapter Five: Touching 27

Chapter Six: Free Will 29

Chapter Seven: Hind sight 33

Chapter Eight: Gifts...37

Chapter Nine: Success...43

Conclusion...45

Glossary of Terms We Have Heard 47

Reviews 49

Dedication

To every parent who has preceded me or will come after and uttered the words "children should come with a manual" or "it's not like they came with a manual". To every parent who has done or is trying to do the best they know how, with their child, and felt unsure if it was right or enough.

To every grandparent able to see their mistakes, by watching their child interact with the grandchildren, and mimicking what they learned from you.

My hope is that this little book will be of assistance, encouragement and comfort.

> 2 Timothy 3:16–17   Every scripture is God breathed and righteousness that each person who belongs to God may be complete, thoroughly equipped for every good work.

> Psalm 9:10   Those who know Your name will put their trust in You; for You, Lord, have not forsaken those who seek You.

Preface

Children actually do come with a manual, and a guide on its use. The manual is the Holy bible, and the guide is the Holy Spirit.

Like most manuals, often they are not opened and read until there is a problem. If you are like most of us, when we get something new we just start using or enjoying it, before we have read the manual to understand what it requires to keep it at maximum performance.

Often by the time we read it, we have made mistakes, gotten frustrated, experienced hurt and or fear, regrets…and the list goes on. We are encouraged to train up, love, discipline, and forgive our children at the least, the manual they come with helps us to know the right way to do that.

This little book is intended to highlight some of the things we are to teach them and how to find the help we need, it will also contain some specific scriptures to help and how they apply. My hope is that we will be reminded, we have a support team available to help us, God our heavenly father, mentor parents, prayer teams, and the teachers of both sabbath and Sunday schools.

> Prov. 22:6 Train up a child in the way he should go and when he is old he will not depart from it. (KJV)

> Ps. 127:3 Behold, children are a gift of the Lord, the fruit of the womb is a reward. The king James translation calls children a heritage instead of a gift. Personally I like that verbiage.

> Prov. 17:6 Grandchildren are the crown of old men, and the glory of sons is their fathers.

> Prov. 23:24 the father of the righteous shall greatly rejoice and he that begetteth a wise child shall have great joy in him

Introduction

The following pages are the first of several projects to share some insights about children, parenting and the presence of God our creator and father, in our daily lives. It is this writers opinion that children are one of Gods greatest gifts in our life, the time we are able to spend with them helps us relate to God as his children. Through our children we learn the pain that God experiences when we, his children, make wrong choices and the joy he experiences when we make good choices.

As parents we are given the opportunity to help children through their struggles and demonstrate that we are always there for them just as God is always there for us. It is my hope that all who read these works find encouragement and reminder of who we are in Christ, children of the one true God, our father, our abba.

The bibles used as reference in these writings are:

- King James Translation
- New Standard school and library reference Bible (red letter edition)
- New American Standard (Ryrie study bible)

Chapter One

EVERY CHILD IS A GIFT

Every child is a heritage or gift created by God, preplanned and delivered to us with a body a spirit and a free will. Every child will, through the nature our creator gave them, be touched by and touch others, they each have a purpose for which they were created. Every child will make a difference from the beginning even those born or not before full term. Hearts and lives are touched and changed from the moment of conception to the end of their journey, no matter how long that might be. (this is a truth revealed)

Worst conception scenario is that of rape, but even a child from this event is a gift for someone, if not the victim then possibly for a childless couple who long for a child and are unable to conceive. Only God knows how to turn such a horrific happening into a blessing. A child that comes from an undesired choice of one can become a joy and blessing for another. Every child has a potential for good under the care and teaching that God has outlined in his manual. And every victim can with Gods help find both healing and peace. No gift should be discarded. If this child is not meant to spend time on this earth it is God and God alone that should make that determination. It must always be his will and not ours that matters, it is God who gives and should be him that takes away. Having said that, let me also share that if you ended a child's life at any point, and are willing to humble yourself and ask forgiveness from God, he is faithful and able to recognize remorse and will forgive you. God's peace, healing and the return of his joy can follow that forgiveness. Let us nurture-embrace-and love each child so they can maximize the success of their journey through this life, no matter how long that journey might be. Let us be faithful to raise them up in the Lord in accordance to his manual, teaching them to follow in his ways and to love him with their whole being.

Here are some places to see first hand how our Lord feels about children.

- Gift—Gen. 21:8 and the child grew and was weaned, and Abraham made a great feast on the day that Isaac was weaned. (they celebrated the gift of a child in their old age.)
- Delightful—Jer. 31:20 "Is Ephraim my dear son? Is he a delightful child? Indeed, as often as I have spoken against him, I certainly still remember him; therefore,

my heart yearns for him; I will surely have mercy on him;" declares the Lord.

- Called a child to life—Luke 8:54-55 He, however, took her by the hand and called, saying "child arise" and her spirit returned, and she rose immediately; and He gave orders that something be given her to eat.

- Heaven belongs—Matt. 19:14 But Jesus said "let the children alone, and do not hinder them from coming to me; for the kingdom of heaven belongs to such as these."

- God our father, Christ our advocate—1John 2:1 my little children, I am writing these things to you that you may not sin. And if anyone sins, we have an advocate with the Father, Jesus Christ the righteous.

- Compassion for a child—Ps. 103:13 Just as a father has compassion on his children, so the Lord has compassion on those who fear him.

You should know that fear in this text does not mean afraid of, it means to revere and value him.

Chapter Two

WHY AM I HERE?

We were created by God to love, learn, to be prepared and taught. Guided by the Holy Spirit we are to fellowship with God and one another, sharing, praying for and growing in our love of Christ, to glorify our Father in heaven.

Life eternal with the Father and our savior is an amazing and powerful existence beyond anything we can perceive or even imagine. The Bible teaches us how to get there and why we want to be there and what the alternative is. Our time on this earth, our journey in this life is a time for learning, loving, growing and serving. We should learn of Gods great love for us, his desire for our lives, Christ's sacrifice for our sins and why it was necessary, how to receive his gift of salvation and what that means for us, how to enjoy a relationship with him, how to receive the Holy spirit, how to serve others and touch their lives for Christs sake and to the Glory of God.

The opportunity to live with our creator forever is offered to everyone, but sadly, not all will accept it or Him.

How long our journey is depends on how fast we learn, how many detours we take and how often our own will gets in the way. For some the journey is short, seconds or hours, for some the journey is long, only God knows what the timing is and when we will be ready to rest and await his return, so we can join him in the place he has prepared for us.

We are all connected with each other, touching each others lives and through those touches creating changes. We are rarely aware at the time how what we do or say will affect others. When we listen to the leading of the Holy spirit and obey what we are told to do, our effect on others is positive, but sometimes we chose to do our own thing, implement our own will, defying what we should do, unfortunately it doesn't usually turn out well, sometimes the affect is not just negative for others but can even be deadly, let me give you an example.

Q. If you choose to drink or drug and drive, and that action results in the life of another being cut short, was that premature death Gods will?

A. ABSOLUTELY NOT, your will made that decision.

Q. Were a lot of lives, including your own, affected by the choice you made?

A. DEFINITELY

Q. Did he send his spirit, his angels, his people to tell you not to do it?

A. ABSOLUTELY YES- ALWAYS he is after all our father and wants only what is best for us. He wants us to be joyful, peaceful, loving and happy. He wants us to make good choices and tries to guide us.

Q. Did you ignore his voice, turn away, rebel, argue, insist you were fine, get angry at the suggestion you might be impaired, what ever?

A. OBVIOUSLY.

Q. Do you have a clue how many life journeys have been altered by your choice (including your own)?

A. probably NOT

We are all here for the same purpose, to learn, to love, and to serve. Your manual, the Bible, will teach you about your Creator, his love for us, how to draw close to him, what it means to fear Him, what he expects from us, what we can expect of Him and how to care for the bodies he has given us. He wants our love and the opportunity to lavish his love on us, but he wants us to do everything willingly and freely.

As children, we are given the ability to feel the tug of the spirit and we count on our parents to teach us what it means. The more familiar we are with the holy word of God, through study, fellowship, and Biblical teachers the faster we learn; that through Christ our savior comes our salvation, the baptism of the Holy spirit, and the ability to develop a lasting relationship with Christ, and to grow stronger in our faith in God. We will touch lives of others, be touched by others and the circle of contact grows, like tossing a pebble in a pond. It is important therefore that our touching is lead by God, that the ears of our heart are tuned to hear his voice. It is important that we now his word and his ways so we can recognize when someone tries to deceive or fool us.

All of mankind were designed for an eternal life with Him, but were also given a free will and as much as it breaks his heart to know it, not all will choose to experience life and worship with Him. Some will turn their backs and walk away from him, separating themselves from his love and kindness forever, choosing instead to follow the great deceiver. The Bible tells us in Revelations that most will be deceived, and how sad that is. Pray that no one we love and know is counted among the most.

My prayer for us all is this, that we have ears that hear, eyes that can see the glory of our Lord and Savior, hearts that are willing to surrender to His perfect will and obey his every word. Amen

Chapter Three

THE TRINITY AND HELPING CHILDREN UNDERSTAND IT

Father: God is the father and the Creator of the world and all living things that it contains as revealed in the book of Genesis, appropriately the first book in your manual the Bible. He created humans, animals, everything that flies, everything in the seas and everything that creeps on the ground and all of these he gave breathe, his spirit, he literally breathed into everything a part of himself to give them life and when they die, that breathe or spirit returns to him. Gen.1:1-2:25

Holy spirit: This is a part of God our Creator that was present in the beginning, Gen. 1:2 says he moved over the waters, He was used in the creation of life, (called the breathe of life)Gen. 2:5. The Holy spirit overshadowed Mary at the conception of Jesus, Luke 1:35, he was sent to empower the son of God, Jesus Christ, at his baptism in water, Matt. 3:16. the Holy spirit is sent of God to baptize and empower the born again believer, some times called the spirit of truth or the helper. John 15:26

The Holy spirit was a part of the creation process, used by God to give life to all things, and since the Bible says God breathed him out, he obviously was in God at the time.

Gen. 1:2. Christ says in John 15:26 that he (the spirit) "comes out of the Father". So although the spirit can do work on his own he is never disconnected or out of sync with the will of God, you might say they are of one mind and heart.

Son: At the time of creation Christ was called the Word and was with God just as the spirit was and according to John 1:1-3 nothing was created without him. How amazing is that? He Christ was with God, and was God from the beginning, and out of his love for us he left his heavenly home, authority, and power to come to earth as a babe, taking on human form and existence to teach, by example and to sacrifice himself in our place, taking on himself the punishment for our sins. His sacrifice makes it possible not only for our salvation but also to one day live with him again eternally in paradise and the new Jerusalem. This relationship between Christ, God, Holy spirit, and us has got to be considered one of the greatest mysteries of God, talk about unlimited love, wow.

When the child Jesus was physically born of God through the power of the spirit which came over Mary, He Jesus became the first born son of the most high God, The I am, the Alpha and the Omega. Jesus is our king, the heir supreme and by his grace and his sacrifice we are allowed to become his adopted brothers and sisters, but we should remember that just as Christ served Gods will so should we serve Christ.

If we confess our sins, and ask Christ into our own hearts and lives, believing that he is indeed the Son of the living God, we can also request to receive the baptism of the Holy spirit. The Spirit is from God but comes to use through Christ Jesus. His spirit is added to our own and we will be made a new, so that his spirit can live in us. Our brother Jesus Christ gave his very life so that we could be called his brothers and sisters. It wasn't anything we did or even deserve, but out of his grace and love for us.

John3:16 For God so loved the world that He gave his only begotten Son, that whoever believes Him should not perish, but have ever lasting life.

John 4:13,14 Jesus answered and said to her,(a Samaritan woman)'everyone who drinks of this water will thirst again; but whoever drinks of the water that I shall give him shall never thirst; but the water I give him shall become in him a well of water springing up to eternal life."

Acts 16:31 and they said, "believe in the Lord Jesus, and you shall be saved, you and your household".

Phil 2:11 That every tongue should confess that Jesus Christ is Lord, to the glory of l God the father.

John 8:26 and John 8:38 Christ reveals his previous time with the father and the truths He is sharing with the Jews and us. These two scriptures have not only blessed me but also caused many hours of contemplation as I consider how great His love for us is. Out of his great love for us he left the physical presence of God temporarily, (maintaining his spiritual connection) and coming to teach us and share the truths he learned while present with God, the father, so we too can experience a life with both him (Jesus) and God for eternity. Wow, three persons all separate and yet one.

Chapter Four

POWER OF THE SPIRIT

The power of the Holy spirit is so extensive that the scriptures in your manual number in the hundreds. From these we can, through study learn a great deal about it, here area few:

- 1Cor. 2:10-11 tells us about how much he knows of both God and man (intelligent)
- Eph. 4:30 tells us he has feelings
- John 14:26 tell us he teaches
- 1 Cor. 12:11 he has a will
- Romans 8:14 says he guides us
- Acts 13:4 he commissions men
- Romans 8:26 says he intercedes
- Gen. 6:3 he restrains
- John 15:26 & 2 Peter 1:21 says he speaks

- Acts 10:19-21 he can be obeyed
- Acts 5:3 says he can be lied to
- Acts 7:51 he can be resisted
- Ps. 51:11 he can be reverenced
- Matt. 12:31 says he can be blasphemed
- Eph. 4:30 says he can be grieved
- Heb. 10:29 he can be outrages
- John 14:16 he can be your helper, comforter

As you can see the Spirit is not only real but powerful, what a blessing that God would send him to indwell in us. It is important that we hold his power in reverence and respect that he is sent of God for a specific and powerful purpose in our lives, the more open we are to the power and influence in our lives the better our journey on this earth will go.

We are warned in Eph. 4:30-32 And do not grieve th Holy Spirit of God, by whom you were sealed for the day of redemption. Let all bitterness and wrath and anger and clamor and slander be put away from you along with malice, and be kind to one another, tender hearted, forgiving, each other, just as God in Christ also has forgiven you.

Ps. 51:10 tells us that the Spirit can be renewed which tells me that if we are not mindful it can be in need of renewal, taken from us or hidden maybe.

1Cor. 12:4 Tells us that the spirit can provide a variety of gifts according to the needs for the common good.

2Cor. 13:14 tells us that we can fellowship with the Holy spirit, how cool is that. 1 Thess. 5:19 do not quench the spirit. do not despise prophetic utterances

We can recognize the presence of the Holy spirit in others by the fruits the spirit produces. We read in Gal. 5:22-23 and the Bible says "But the fruit of the Spirit is love, joy, peace, patience, kindness, goodness, faithfulness, gentleness, self-control against such things there is no law.

Gal. 5:16-17 But I say walk by the Spirit and you will not carry out the desires of the flesh, For the flesh sets its desire against the Spirit, and the Spirit against the flesh; for these are in opposition to one another, so that you may not do the things that you please.

Can you see the importance of studying your manual to learn about all of the tools and helps available so that you can succeed. Gods word is overflowing with useful information, helps and warnings.

Chapter Five

TOUCHING

We, everyone of us, touch and impact the lives of others. We say or do something that changes or influences someone else. We don't see it, think about it or take responsibility for it, but the fact is we do. What we do, or don't do, what we say or don't say, what we are silent about or speak out about, sometimes even our attitude or body language can have an impact on others.

We can be given the Holy Spirit to guide us in how to use this incredible ability to better the world we live in and move ourselves and others along on the journey. How sad it is when we receive the spirit and then fail to listen to it and obey its direction. How much smoother and more productive when we do listen to the spirit and obey as we are directed.

I am reminded of an example of this thing that happened in our lives. My husband and I stopped for dinner out, which we usually reserved for special occasions, since we were headed home from my second successful eye surgery which meant I would no longer be blind, we felt a celebration was in order. The place we chose was one that we had enjoyed on previous occasions, but this time it was different. The waitress who greeted and seated us was well groomed and appeared pleasant, but very soon after we were seated it became apparent that she would rather have been some where else, several of the customers were commenting on her attitude and curtness. We too started to feel defensive, when the spirit reminded us that what she needed from us was kindness and maybe prayer for what ever was causing her pain, so in obedience when we prayed over our meal, we lifted her in prayer as well, and at the end of our meal we left her a larger than normal tip, because we heard others say they would not be tipping her. I was offered a comment card by the counter person but as I reached for it a still small voice told me not now. I remembered that in scripture we are taught that when others treat us poorly we are to repay them with kindness, so we smiled and left. When we got home I did send her a card to tell her that she had waited on us and that we were concerned and would be keeping her in our prayers. It was a kinder way to touch her life. When we listen to and follow the leading of God's Holy Spirit, the out come is always better.

We are to listen, wait to hear and then obey, I like to follow up with thanking God for the intervention and guidance.

Chapter Six

FREE WILL

We have all been given the right and ability to make our own choices in life, it is called our free will, we were given this from a loving Father who does not desire a forced or fear based love from us, but rather a freely given love for and devotion to him. Even the angels were given free will, which is what allowed some of them to seek their own way. It is this freedom that sets us apart from other created things. Scripture tells us that if we choose not to worship and praise Gods name, even the rocks will cry out to him. Pretty sad that our loving Father would have to hear the praise of a rock instead of the praises of his beloved. Free will is a characteristic that we share with both Christ and the Holy Spirit. Christ our redeemer in his wisdom chose to surrender his will to God, allowing God to choose for him what should be done, when in the garden of Gethsemane he said "not my will Father but thine be done.

We as carnal man can be kind of stubborn and willful, wanting what we want when we want it and pitching a fit when things don't go as we think they should, but always this attitude creates more difficulty than necessary. We want to handle things our own way, be in charge, masters of our own destiny, what a joke that truly is on us. I heard some one say one time that if you want to make God laugh, tell him your plans, I think it might be more true than not, as I have come to realize how little we really know about what is best for us. We as a people in general are easily lead astray and ready to believe the lies of the deceiver. I have learned that the only advice or guidance of value is provided by the Holy Spirit and confirmed in the scriptures. If we are not listening to and guided by the Spirit of God we are likely to wield our will like an untrained swordsman and that usually results in collateral damage, which in turn creates more need and opportunity to listen, which we usually don't, so we spend a lot of unnecessary energy trying to correct the mess we have made. Through it all, including the bad attitude and bad choices, Jesus still loves us and stands ready to help when we finally do ask.

I am sure that the heart of God breaks a little each time we brashly disregard his good will for us and do things that hurt ourselves or others. I know that as a parent, my heart breaks a little each time I witness a bad choice that will bring a negative consequence. What joy he must surely experience when we do in fact find our way back to his easier and planned pathway for us.

He (our creator) gave us a free will out of great love for us and a great desire to be loved by us, his children. He desires that we freely love and obey his commands so he can spend more time with us, like eternity. He is our perfect example of how to love in that even when we do make mistakes, as we all do, he is still pulling for us to seek forgiveness so he can give it, and while he waits he is right beside us as we endure he consequences of our choices, using the power of his spirit to convict our hearts and encourage our remorse.

It seems to me that wisdom is evidenced when we yield our will to him and say "not my will Father but yours be done in my life".

Chapter Seven

HIND SIGHT

Have you ever found yourself in a situation where you had the feeling that what you were about to do was wrong? You had a feeling or a sense that is was not a good idea, maybe you even had someone tell you not to go that way or that's not a good idea, but you chose to do it anyway. Later you recognize that the decision you made was bad and had some uncomfortable results. It is usually at this point that we say things like, I should have known better, or something told me that was a bad idea, or I should have trusted my instincts, that is called Hind sight. The term means that when we look back on the situation we see it with new clarity or light.

Sometimes we go through the same thing repeatedly because we continue to make the same errors in our behavior over and over again, not listening to the Spirit for warnings or guidance. We never allow enough distance from the problem to be able to see the whole of it clearly. We hear ourselves asking why am I still going through the same thing. And not recognizing that we are not changing anything and yet we are expecting a different result, so around and around we go. If we are ever able to step back, to see with more clarity the right direction, and make the appropriate changes then we say to ourselves, why didn't I see that or I should have known that, bingo, hind sight.

Let me share with you, one of my, hindsight moments; When I became a born again Christian, a loving man gave me a bible and told me I would need this if I truly wanted to have a close relationship with the Lord. Naturally I was thrilled, but like most people with a new gift I just jumped right in using it, didn't bother to browse all the pages to see what it had to offer, No I didn't. I began reading the Bible like any book front to back. I will admit it was a little over whelming at first, then a Christian mentor at church ask me if he could write something in it for me, he wrote the following; how to gain the most from your Bible; read it for knowledge- pray over it for wisdom- believe it for salvation- and live it for righteousness. Wow I can do that. Later the church pastor shared this with me, in reference to the old and new testaments; the new is in the old contained- the old is in the new explained- the new is in the old concealed- the old is in the new revealed.

At this point I was truly confused and struggling. I went back to what my mentor had written and at that point I prayed over it for wisdom. It was at this point that the spirit led me to leaf through and try to find all of the books, since the pastor had preached on revelations recently I thought that is a good place to start. I found the book of Revelations only had 22 chapters but there were still a lot of pages behind it. In the back pages of my bible I discovered a lot of amazing tools to help me study. Things like the harmony of the gospels, a section on doctrines of the Bible, one on the inspiration of the Bible, how we got the Bible, miracles of Jesus, a topical study, index to principal subjects, and a concordance and maps- lots of maps. I felt like a child that just learned to read, suddenly a new clarity had been given me. My hindsight moment was in learning that all of that information had been there all along, and I should have known to peruse the whole of the manual early on. Thank you God for the people and the spirit that you provided in my time of need, what a blessing it has been.

Chapter Eight

GIFTS

We are all given gifts, or talents if you will, by our Creator God. The number of gifts and the degree of them will vary from person to person as determined by God through the Spirit of God. Some people are given more that one talent but all are expected to use the talents they are given. You could possibly be given one and later have another added as well. We do not always readily recognize the talent we have but often it is recognizable to others. We are usually pretty amazed when some one points out a gift or talent that we are unaware of, or didn't think of as a talent but rather just something that we did naturally. Some gifts are readily recognized like music, the ability to sing beautifully or to play an instrument, but what ever the talent, it still usually requires some development or training to perfect and grow it. And since it comes from God it makes since that it should be used to glorify and honor him.

Just imagine how different and amazing it would be if each of us tried to see the gifts and talents in others, if we sought out their good qualities and abilities and pointed them out to them. Imagine if no one was ever jealous of the talents of another but found joy in the gifts that others have to offer and delighted in knowing our father was being honored and glorified. Unfortunately sometimes our jealousy over the talents of another can blind us to our own talent, and let me add at this point that no one talent has more value than another, all are important and crucial to the whole body of believers and the glorifying of our heavenly Father, all talents and gifts are given to edify and bless others.

We all like to hear things that offer hope and encourage us and yes even the ability to encourage is a gift, so lets take a look at some of the gifts that the Bible talks about and as we read each one I challenge you to think about who you might know that has that gift.

- Love is a gift, the ability to love and demonstrate love through our speech and actions allows those we encounter to feel accepted, valued and welcome.

- Faith is a gift, our faith in God makes our prayers for others more affective and encourages others when we express with confidence that our God can handle what ever comes. Faith in God also creates peace for the believer, as they accept His assurance of love, concern, compassion, mercy, and grace for them. One of the good things about faith is that if is not deceived by what it sees.

- Charity is a gift, the willingness to sacrifice our desires for the needs of others is an act of charity. Most people think of charity as a monetary thing but charity can also be putting things you would like to do aside to do for another what they need done, setting their needs before your own.

- Healing is a gift, some people can lay hands on you and through the Holy spirit, by the power of God can heal the body. Others have been given the ability to use herbs and foods to heal others and some use the gift of prayer to both heal and comfort the spirit of another.

- Visions are a gift, the Bible offers a lot of examples where teachings, fore warnings, directions and answers were revealed through visions. In all cases a true vision will never disagree with Gods teachings, nor will it be harmful to another. If you have ever experienced a vision or known someone who has, they are powerful.

- Dreams are a gift, there are a lot of people with whom God uses dreams as a way to communicate. When you think about men that God used in mighty ways or where dreams played a key role most often our mind jumps directly to Danial. I can't help wondering if God uses dreams because we are asleep and can't argue with him about what he says, I am just saying, naturally I am thinking of my own behavior here.

- Speaking in tongues is a gift, the ability to speak in a language that is unfamiliar to you, This is less common than some but powerful in evangelism. Some believe this refers only to the use of a heavenly language, but a pastor of mine personally experienced this gift at a gathering in a foreign country, where usually interpreters are used and you have to wait for the message to be translated, A man got up to speak and our pastor understood and heard everything in his own tongue. When he expressed gratitude for the message and the kindness of them using his own language to deliver it he learned that the speaker wasn't aware he was heard in English. At Pentecost the Bible says the disciples delivered a message to all the people and each heard the message in their own tongue and were amazed.

- Discernment is a gift that allows us to recognize hidden or disguised things and spirits. The Bible tells us that Christ could discern the presence of demonic spirits and call them out. Discernment can allow us to know or recognize falsehoods as well

- Teaching is a gift, it is a special ability to help someone else understand something, to explain things in such a way that the one listening gets a clarity they didn't have before.

- Preaching is a gift and helps people receive the gospel message with a new openness in their hearts and minds. A good preacher has the ability to reach us in our brokenness without making us feel less worthy of grace.

More gifts are some of the ones covered in the chapter on the Holy Spirit. The gifts are many, my challenge to you is to look hard for gifts of God in not only yourself but in others, when necessary reveal them and always encourage their development.

We serve a gracious and loving God who is willing to give to us more than our hearts and minds can imagine. James 1:17 says Every good thing bestowed and every perfect gift is from above, coming down from the Father of lights, with whom there is no variation or shifting shadow. We serve a constant and consistent God, Hallelujah!

Chapter Nine

SUCCESS

You will know that you have met your goal when your manual has become your greatest companion and most valued possession, and your children feel confident to leave your home, take a spouse and begin a life of their own. Double blessing will come if they feel comfortable to take on the task of children of their own, your grandchildren.

Joy will fill your heart as you watch them interact with those children, sharing what they learned from your guidance and using the same manual you did. You will experience the next level of joy as you enjoy their laughter, tender hugs, sweet smiles and try to answer there questions, like how come the sky is blue where does the sun go down to?

Total satisfaction and rejoicing comes in seeing your grown children living godly lives, walking in the spirit, obedient to the word and glorifying God, Christ and the Holy spirit. Joy will fill your heart because you know that even when this earthly life is over you can be reunited with them at the second coming of our Lord.

Congratulations.

Conclusion

As I complete this book I am lead to share with you some of the things I have learned during the process.

- God has a sense of humor and enjoys laughter, God can use anyone to do anything he wants done, no matter what they perceive to be limitations, so long as they are willing to submit to his will.

- I still have a lot to learn, my training on this earth is not yet done.

- We will be writing more books together and these books are only tools.

- Obedience, even when we don't understand what he is doing or why is crucial.

- Listening for his voice is important, hearing what he is saying and yielding is a difference maker.

- If I submit wholly to his will for my heart and life he will reveal my tendency to interfere or assume and help me get back on track.

- God is a multi-task expert and we seldom if ever understand or see how He is working all things together for our good.

- If we are willing to obey, even when we don't understand, He is faithful to reveal the pieces and the whole they created for what ever is being done, but always in his perfect timing, and that timing is rarely the same as what we think it should be, but it is always perfect.

- Gods love for us is greater than anything we can possibly understand and every small detail in our lives are important to him, nothing is too small to bring before His throne.

Glossary of Terms We Have Heard

Gift of visions: Little previews of things to come and possibilities open to us. They come from God when our hearts are willing to receive and obey what he asks of us, not a reward but rather a result of obedience.

Gift of dreams: are often a means for the spirit of God to communicate things to us, that our preoccupied and full minds can't listen too while we are awake.

Grand desires: We often think that we must do something large and grandiose to serve God. We even gauge our quality of service to him by what we think in others to be great. But if we are honest with ourselves these desires are usually for selfish recognition (like the Pharisees} A true grand desire is to do what God wants done, so that all of the glory and credits go to God alone. In reality everyone can serve God where ever they are and whoever they are, if they desire to do so.

Grand design: Gods pleasure and purpose for us and our lives. Simply stated we were created to love God and to be loved by God. Our demonstration of that love is in living an obedient life, sharing his love with our fellow man, helping and praying for one another, being followers not just believers in Christ, because remember that even Satan believes in Christ and God.

Revelation: A truth of God revealed to mankind through the power of the Holy Spirit

Adversary: usually in biblical reference this is one of names and focus of Satan, also known as liar, deceiver, destroyer. He is ruthless and he is wrong but he is also very real, his delight is in those who doubt he is real as they make easy victims of his treachery.

Guide book for life eternal: The Holy Bible

Reviews

Children Do Come With A Manual

Top reviews from the United States

 Michelle

⭐⭐⭐⭐⭐ **Exciting to read**

Reviewed in the United States on July 4, 2023

"Children Do Come With A Manual" is a comprehensive manual for life's journey. The book emphasizes the importance of reading the Bible daily and learning from its promises, warnings, and examples. It's an empowering resource for anyone seeking guidance and fulfillment in their lives.

Helpful	Report

 Nicole

⭐⭐⭐⭐⭐ **A Guidebook for Parenting and Beyond**

Reviewed in the United States on June 22, 2023

Children Do Come With A Manual is an invaluable guidebook for parents and anyone seeking wisdom in life. Elizabeth Len Wai emphasizes the importance of using the Bible as a daily manual for raising children and navigating through life's challenges. The book offers practical insights, historical context, and valuable lessons from scriptures. It's a must-read for those who want to raise their children to be followers of Christ and live fulfilling lives.

Helpful	Report

Kelly

★★★★★ **A Powerful Reminder of God's Gifts and Love**

Reviewed in the United States on June 15, 2023

In "Children Do Come with a Manual," Elizabeth Len Wai beautifully reminds us that children are God's creation and a precious gift. With her wisdom rooted in biblical teachings, Len Wai guides parents and grandparents in understanding their role as spiritual mentors. Her emphasis on the Trinity, the Holy Spirit's work, and the power of love provides a solid foundation for raising godly children. This heartfelt book serves as a constant reminder of the many gifts bestowed upon Christian believers and offers practical insights for navigating the joys and challenges of parenting.

Helpful | Report

 Scarlett Smith

★★★★★ **Enlightening and Informative!**

Reviewed in the United States on May 25, 2023

The author asserts that their is a MANUAL for childrenand that is the .... HOLY BIBLE! The author believes that through bible study , parents and grandparents learn what to teach their children. The author believes that when parents use the bible as their source of guidance the rewards comes " in seeing your grown children living godly lives and I believe what the author is saying is so true! This is truly enlightening for first time parents like me! ***

Helpful | Report

 Brooklyn H.

★★★★★ **An Empowering Resource for Parents and Caregivers**

Reviewed in the United States on June 19, 2023

"Children Do Come with a Manual" by Elizabeth Len Wai is a powerful and empowering book for parents and caregivers. This book serves as a practical reference and reminder of the profound impact parents can have on their children's lives. It's a must-read for anyone seeking to navigate the joys and challenges of parenting with a solid spiritual foundation.

Emma Gilford

☆☆☆☆☆ **Building Strong Foundations**

Reviewed in the United States on July 27, 2023

Elizabeth Len Wai's "Children Do Come With A Manual" is an indispensable tool for parents and children's ministry workers, emphasizing the importance of biblical principles in raising children who walk in the ways of Christ. This book has enriched my understanding and approach to children's ministry at our church.

Helpful	⋮ Report

 Valarie

☆☆☆☆☆ **A Nurturing Guide for Expectant Parents**

Reviewed in the United States on July 11, 2023

"Children Do Come With A Manual" by Elizabeth Len Wai is an invaluable resource that every expectant parent should have on their bookshelf. As we eagerly anticipate the arrival of our little one, this book serves as a comforting companion, guiding us to embrace the wisdom and guidance found in the Bible. Wai's perspective on the Bible as "Basic Instructions Before Leaving Earth" resonates deeply with me. Through her insightful unpacking of scriptures, she sheds light on the profound lessons and revelations they hold. This manual goes beyond the usual parenting guides, offering a holistic approach to raising a child rooted in faith, love, and character development.

Helpful	⋮ Report

 Amy

☆☆☆☆☆ **The Bible: A Parent's Manual**

Reviewed in the United States on July 29, 2023

A must-have for parents, this book reminds us that the Bible is the ultimate manual for navigating the joys and challenges of parenting.

Helpful	⋮ Report

Liam

★★★★★ **Raising Children with the Bible**
Reviewed in the United States on July 30, 2023

Elizabeth Len Wai's book beautifully emphasizes the importance of using the Bible as a daily guide in raising children to lead fulfilling and successful lives.

Helpful | Report

Ella Go

★★★★★ **A Spiritual Roadmap for Parenting**
Reviewed in the United States on July 11, 2023

As we eagerly await the arrival of our little one, "Children Do Come With A Manual" by Elizabeth Len Wai has become our trusted companion in this journey of parenthood. Wai's thoughtful exploration of the Bible as a guidebook for raising children resonates deeply with our faith-centered approach to life. This manual offers much more than practical advice; it delves into the heart and soul of parenting, illuminating the divine principles and teachings that can shape our child's character. Wai's thorough understanding of scripture allows her to beautifully communicate the intent behind our existence, our history of rebellion, and the path to restoration.

Helpful | Report

Wendell

★★★★★ **The Bible Unpacked in a Refreshing Way**
Reviewed in the United States on July 7, 2023

Elizabeth Len Wai's "Children Do Come With A Manual" unpacks the Bible in a refreshing and relatable manner. This book goes beyond traditional manuals, exploring the origins, intentions, and history of humanity's relationship with God. It provides guidance on parenting, relationships, personal growth, and more. The author's emphasis on daily engagement with scriptures reminds us of the Bible's relevance in our everyday lives.

Helpful | Report

Francesca Miller

★★★★★ **A Little Book with Profound Wisdom**
Reviewed in the United States on June 16, 2023

Elizabeth Len Wai's "Children Do Come with a Manual" may be a brief read, but its wisdom runs deep. With grace and clarity, Len Wai reminds us that the Holy Bible is the ultimate guide for parents and caregivers. Her insights on free will and the choice to love God resonate profoundly, offering a framework for navigating the complexities of raising children. This book is a perfect companion for anyone seeking scriptural wisdom and reminders to lean on during the journey of parenting. It's a true gem that will enrich the lives of both children and adults.

Helpful | Report

Andrew M.

★★★★★ **Unlocking the Secrets of the Bible**
Reviewed in the United States on June 23, 2023

Elizabeth Len Wai's "Children Do Come With A Manual" is a thought-provoking exploration of the Bible's teachings. It offers practical guidance for daily living, covering areas such as relationships, self-improvement, and discernment. Whether you're a parent or simply seeking spiritual wisdom, this manual is a valuable resource.

Mia

★★★★★ **Timeless Wisdom for Parents**

Reviewed in the United States on July 31, 2023

This book is a valuable resource for parents, offering timeless wisdom from the Scriptures to help them navigate the rewarding journey of parenthood.

Helpful | Report

Calvin

★★★★★ **Unlocking the Power of Scripture in Parenting**

Reviewed in the United States on August 4, 2023

As a children's ministry volunteer, I highly recommend "Children Do Come With A Manual" for parents seeking to raise children rooted in faith. Elizabeth Len Wai's emphasis on daily Bible study and its application to parenting aligns perfectly with our church's mission.

Helpful | Report

Kathleen

★★★★★ **Timely read**

Reviewed in the United States on July 11, 2023

"Children Do Come With A Manual" by Elizabeth Len Wai is a heartfelt and faith-centered book that has become my go-to resource as an expectant parent. In a world filled with conflicting advice, Wai's emphasis on using the Bible as a manual for parenting brings a sense of clarity and purpose to this incredible journey.

As I delve into the scriptures revealed in this book, I am inspired by the depth of wisdom they contain. Wai expertly unpacks the biblical teachings, exploring not only the practical aspects of child-rearing but also the spiritual and moral values that shape a child's character. Her reminder that the Bible is a comprehensive guide for life resonates deeply with my desire to raise my child in accordance with God's plan.

Helpful | Report

Sabrina M.

★★★★★ **A Roadmap to Raising Faithful Children**

Reviewed in the United States on July 27, 2023

"Children Do Come With A Manual" is an excellent resource for parents and children's ministry leaders alike. Elizabeth Len Wai's insights into biblical guidance and nurturing a love for God's Word among kids have been a valuable asset in our church community.

Helpful | Report

Sandy

★★★★★ **A Testament to Unwavering Faith and Love**

Reviewed in the United States on June 20, 2023

This book is a valuable resource for teaching children important spiritual concepts, empowering them to make choices based on love and obedience to God's commands. Len Wai's heartfelt writing resonates deeply and leaves readers inspired and encouraged.

Walter

⭐⭐⭐⭐⭐ **The Ultimate Parenting Guide**

Reviewed in the United States on July 27, 2023

Children Do Come With A Manual is a powerful guide for parents seeking wisdom and guidance from the Bible in raising their children to be followers of Christ.

[Helpful]   Report

 Valarie

⭐⭐⭐⭐⭐ **A Nurturing Guide for Expectant Parents**

Reviewed in the United States on July 11, 2023

"Children Do Come With A Manual" by Elizabeth Len Wai is an invaluable resource that every expectant parent should have on their bookshelf. As we eagerly anticipate the arrival of our little one, this book serves as a comforting companion, guiding us to embrace the wisdom and guidance found in the Bible. Wai's perspective on the Bible as "Basic Instructions Before Leaving Earth" resonates deeply with me. Through her insightful unpacking of scriptures, she sheds light on the profound lessons and revelations they hold. This manual goes beyond the usual parenting guides, offering a holistic approach to raising a child rooted in faith, love, and character development.

[Helpful]   Report

 Karen

⭐⭐⭐⭐⭐ **A Must-Have Resource for Children's Ministry**

Reviewed in the United States on August 2, 2023

"Children Do Come With A Manual" by Elizabeth Len Wai is a valuable companion for parents, providing biblical guidance on raising children to be followers of Christ. As a children's ministry worker, I find this book incredibly insightful in nurturing young hearts in the church.

[Helpful]   Report

 Amy

⭐⭐⭐⭐⭐ **The Bible: A Parent's Manual**

Reviewed in the United States on July 29, 2023

A must-have for parents, this book reminds us that the Bible is the ultimate manual for navigating the joys and challenges of parenting.

[Helpful]   Report

 Gwen

⭐⭐⭐⭐⭐ **A Faith-Filled Guide for Expecting Parents**

Reviewed in the United States on July 11, 2023

What sets this book apart is its holistic approach. Wai addresses a wide range of topics, from nurturing healthy habits and building strong relationships to instilling godly values and discernment. The daily readings and practical tips offer guidance for intentional parenting and personal growth.

"Children Do Come With A Manual" is a must-have resource for expectant parents who seek to create a loving, faith-filled environment for their child. Wai's heartfelt words and biblical insights will empower you to navigate the challenges of parenting with grace and wisdom.

[Helpful]   Report

 Noah

⭐⭐⭐⭐⭐ **Comprehensive Guide for Parenting**

Reviewed in the United States on July 31, 2023

An insightful and comprehensive manual, Children Do Come With A Manual covers everything from practical advice to spiritual guidance for parents seeking to raise godly children.

[Helpful]   Report

Reviews

Parenting: It Isn't Hard If You Keep Your Eyes on the Mentor, God, Our Heavenly Father

The US Review of Books
Professional Reviews for the People

I loved this book! It has great information that directly correlates to quoted scripture. It took me back, not only to when I was a child but later when I became a parent and a grandparent and helped me to understand years later what I may not have been so clear about then. It made me laugh with personal accounts of the author's experience, whom by the way I know personally, great spiritual woman, as it was many I had myself with my children. Easy to read and understand plain English with a down to earth style, from a self-proclaimed "regular person". Mrs. LenWai has brought us a great reference to God's way of seeing the parenting experience for this time and any generation! Thank you Elizabeth and may God continue to bless you and your growing family.

Paulette

This is such an amazing book! She is truthful and honest with every chapter! U can tell that she put her heart and soul into this book and used her relationship with God to help guide her in her writing to encourage others. I cant wait and look forward to reading the next book by this amazing author! This book has truly helped me and gives me hope for the future as I raise my 5 children and help them grow into the kinds of people God wants them to be. Thank you Elizabeth!

Kayla Dellinger

THE US Review of Books

Parenting: It Isn't Hard If You Keep Your Eyes on the Mentor, God, Our Heavenly Father
by Elizabeth Len Wai
Covenant Books, Inc.

book review by Barbara Bamberger Scott

"It is important that parents be good prayer warriors on behalf of the children and when seeking help with them."

An experienced parent offers inspirational advice on childrearing in this sincere, gently amusing, Christian themed manual. When parents make poor choices, family breakdown will be the result; but by setting one's sights high and taking biblical teaching into consideration, author Len Wai believes that we can and will become caregivers to "a new generation of God's children." Most people begin to consider their role as parents after they have conceived, or are planning to conceive, their first child. The role of parent and protector of our offspring will ideally reward us with the protection and care we receive from our children as we age. The generations can share with one another, giving and receiving energy and vision.

Len Wai has created a job description for a parent. Duties include caregiving, nursing, and fashion advisor as well as "leader, confessor, comforter." Benefits include years of emotional ups, downs, challenges, and rewards. God, the law, society, teachers, bosses, and mates will all have expectations on our child. We as parents supply the basics and more, and, in all these endeavors, make the child "the center of our world and the focus of all our attention," a phrase the author stresses through repetition. A parent can expect to have moments of doubt and fear. Len Wai describes her own feelings once she brought her firstborn child home. Initially quite confident, she had a sudden surge of pure panic and called her own mother for reassurance. She gives the reader some ideas of what to expect based on her own experience of diapering, playing simple games, feeling frustrated at times, and taking a much broader view of her surroundings seen from the aspects of safety, space, and time management. Parents must learn to forgive, to understand and teach the difference between right and wrong, honesty and dishonesty, and to present themselves as examples of virtue and love, dispensing discipline when required.

Len Wai writes with apparent ease about a subject that is evidently very important to her, important enough to share with others. Her narrative is peppered with relevant quotations from the Bible, a resource that, she believes, can guide us at all stages of our role as dutiful and caring parents. She willingly makes fun of herself, quoting some of the silly things she has said without thinking. This serves to illustrate that parents are not perfect; parents will make mistakes, but it is important that we think about what we say and what we teach our children.

Parenting continues into our older years as grandparents, as the author well knows. In our later years, she suggests, we get to "revisit old friends like Big Bird, Cookie Monster, Winnie-the-Pooh..." through the eyes and ears of a new generation. Traditional activities like dress-up, hide and seek, drawing pictures, and building sandcastles have not gone out of style, and grandparents can be called on to engage in such playful exercises. Len Wai shares fond memories of growing up in a multigenerational home atmosphere and learning from her elders. These reminiscences, combined with observations garnered from her early challenges with parenting, contribute to her current role as author and advisor. Len Wai conveys a comforting sense of calm and wisdom to her reading audience. She constructs a clever comparison of parenting with kite flying: both require determination, control, and a wish to see our aspirations take flight. Her book appropriately concludes with the challenge, "So let's go fly a kite."

RECOMMENDED by the US Review

Parenting: It Isn't Hard If You Keep Your Eyes on the Mentor, God, Our Heavenly Father
Audible Audiobook – Unabridged

Elizabeth Len Wai (Author), Torii Alaniz (Narrator), Mainspring Books (Publisher)

5.0 ★★★★★ ▾ 2 ratings   See all formats and e

▶ Audible sample

God is the only perfect parent; it is appropriate that we should choose him as our mentor in parenting. A lot of the behavior: irritate us in our child, God has experienced with us - tantrums, questioning, disobedience, defiance, crying, and begging. He experienced them all with us and still calls us his children.

©2019 Elizabeth Len Wai (P)2021 Elizabeth Len Wai

Listening Length	Author	Narrator	Audible release date	Language	Publisher
🎧	✏️	🧑‍🎤	📅	🌐	🏛️
1 hour and 13 minutes	Elizabeth Len Wai	Torii Alaniz	July 20, 2021	English	Mainspring Books

---

Official Review: Parenting by Elizabeth Len Wai
📖 by Oyadeji Okikioluwa » 24 May 2021, 08:22

[Following is an official OnlineBookClub.org review of 'Parenting' by Elizabeth Len Wai.]

Are you aware that parenting can be likened to flying a kite? *Parenting* is a 13-chapter book by Elizabeth Len Wai. The book portrayed the right parenting behaviors to readers while discussing qualities such as love, honesty, truth, and discipline.

The book highlighted the duties involved in parenting. It details the parent's responsibilities to their children and what parents should expect from their children. It then discussed forgiveness and its importance. The author also explained the importance of truth and honesty, the good news of God's unwavering love, the meaning of dedication and baptism, and then encouraged readers to rely on God. She discussed grandparenting, the silly things said in the act, and then likened parenting to flying a kite. As a parent, do you need to acquire knowledge on the best way to nurture your children? Then grab a copy of this book to get what you need and more.

4 out of 4 stars

Share This Review
[icons]

Oyadeji Okikioluwa ●
Posts: 1166
Joined: 31 May 2019, 14:24
Currently Reading:
Bookshelf Size: 964
Reviewer Page:
onlinebookclub.org/reviews/by-orizon.html
Latest Review: *Proverbs 4:7* by Gaidi

The accurate Bible references show it is a well-researched book. They confirmed the author's teachings as thrilling and inspiring. The author's experiences and opportunity of growing up in a multigenerational home did well in enriching the book. Elizabeth Len Wai enjoyed love as a kid, which she encouraged other parents to emulate. I enjoyed the book's diction, as they were spiritual and motivational. It was also simple and easy to understand.

I admire moral values such as honesty, love, forgiveness, faith, and responsibility expressed in the book. Words in the book were a charge and motivation to parents to be their best and do their best in training their children to the topmost standard of both God and society. The part of the book where the author urged parents to "make them (children) the center of your world and the focus of your attention" said it all.

Another part of the book that touched me was when the author explained that God gets hurt when we sin because we will have to face our actions' consequences. There is nothing I dislike in the book. Although I found a few grammatical errors, they did not impede my reading experience. The book exceeded its primary purpose of educating, and I enjoyed the time spent on it. Therefore, I rate it **4 out of 4 stars.**

In conclusion, I recommended this book to Christian homes and parents. I would also recommend it to all adults as there would be a time in our lives when we would become parents or guardians, and lessons picked from this book could be helpful.

******
Parenting

Milton Keynes UK
Ingram Content Group UK Ltd.
UKHW011145010424
440421UK00001B/291

9 781960 946577